1001 Pirate
Things to Spot

Rob Lloyd Jones

Illustrated by Teri Gower

Designed by Teri Gower and Michelle Lawrence
Edited by Anna Milbourne
Digital manipulation by Nick Wakeford

Contents

Things to spot

These pirates are a lively bunch of scurvy sea dogs. They love fighting, partying and searching for buried treasure. Each scene in this book has all kinds of exciting pirate things for you to find and count. There are 1001 things to spot altogether.

Pirate port

6 anchors 5 carthorses 9 baskets of fish 5 parrots in cages 10 Jolly Rogers

3 pirates with peg legs 9 pieces of eight 10 barrels of gunpowder 8 stray dogs 5 pelicans

12   13

Each little picture shows you what to look for in the big picture.

The blue number tells you how many of that thing you need to find.

This is Jack, the cabin boy on the pirate ship. He's always busy doing all the pirates' hard work. See if you can spot him in each scene, and then help him with his treasure hunt on page 30.

Life at sea

1 pirate captain

10 striped T-shirts

7 mops

4 telescopes

5 purple pirate hats

9 rats

7 sacks of grain

10 scrawny chickens

3 ship's cats

5 pirates on
the rigging

The captain's feast

10 ships in bottles 9 mice 7 bowls of stew 6 pineapples 8 chicken legs

 5 pirates with eye patches   **9** lanterns   **10** cups of punch   **5** fat cats   **3** pirates in hammocks

Attack!

10 cutlasses

7 tied-up prisoners

5 fist fights

10 flintlocks

8 blunderbusses

4 men walking the plank

6 parrots shrieking

9 grappling hooks

8 cannons

9 cannonballs

Keeping shipshape

5 saws

10 spotted lizards

7 dice

4 pirates sewing sails

8 ladders

10 woodworms

5 buckets of tar

9 hammers

7 scrubbing brushes

3 campfires

Pirate port

6 anchors 5 carthorses 9 baskets of fish 5 parrots in cages 10 Jolly Rogers

3 pirates with peg legs 9 pieces of eight 10 barrels of gunpowder 8 stray dogs 5 pelicans

Pirate school

10 pirate
school books

7 pirate teachers

6 yellow ropes

7 training boats

5 baby parrots

8 wooden cutlasses

4 training cannons

3 sea charts

10 quills

8 catapults

Pirate races

4 pirates water-skiing

6 turtles

4 pirates diving

10 pirate armbands

9 seagulls

7 dolphins

2 surfboards

8 blue pairs of shorts

1 finishing flag

10 seaweed pom-poms

Treasure island

4 treasure maps 6 toucans 8 coconuts 9 monkeys 10 shovels

2 castaways **7** pickaxes **9** crabs **10** iguanas **1** X-marks-the-spot

Pirate party

10 pirate party hats

4 barrels rolling

3 fiddles

9 flower garlands

5 monkeys dancing

9 plates of
party cakes

7 chinese
lanterns

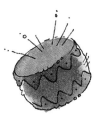
6 drums

8 lollipops

10 pirate
balloons

Monsters of the deep

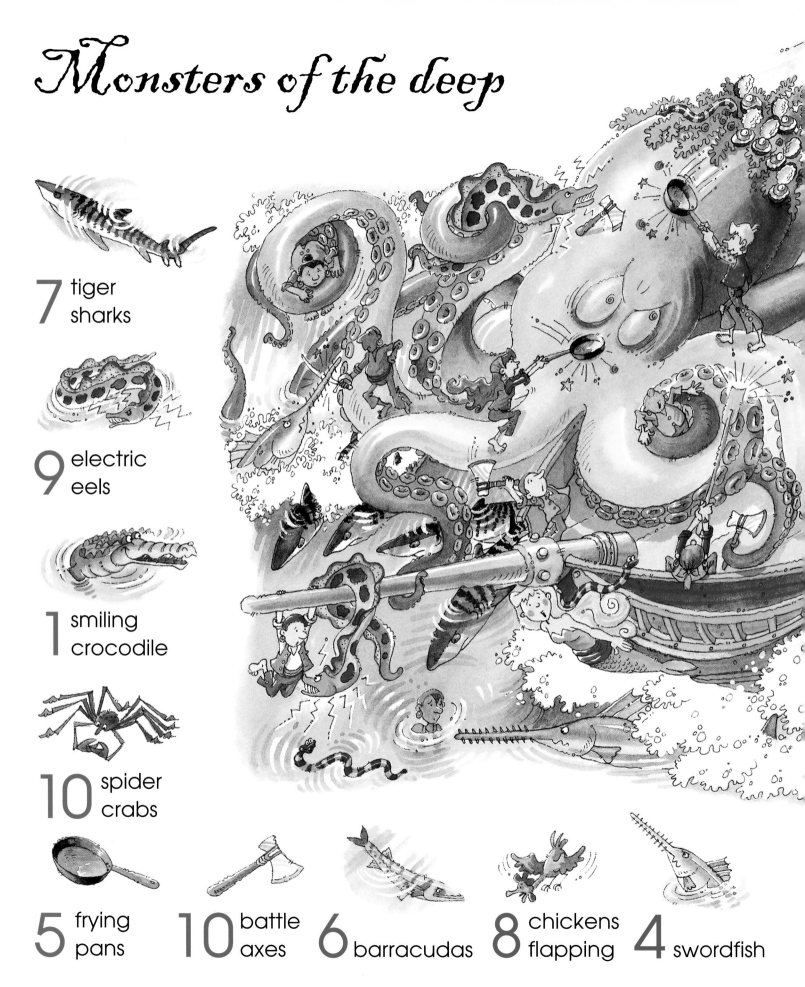

7 tiger sharks

9 electric eels

1 smiling crocodile

10 spider crabs

5 frying pans

10 battle axes

6 barracudas

8 chickens flapping

4 swordfish

10 sea
snakes

Ghost ship

9 skeleton pirates

4 mummies

9 pirate ghosts

5 pirates trembling

6 vultures

24

9 vampire bats

10 giant cobwebs

8 scary spiders

3 creepy coffins

6 vampire rats

Stormy sea

10 men overboard

5 buckets

4 bolts of lightning

8 life rings

5 pirate umbrellas

5 seasick pirates

8 shark fins

9 barrels floating

1 lighthouse

10 pirates in raincoats

Shipwreck

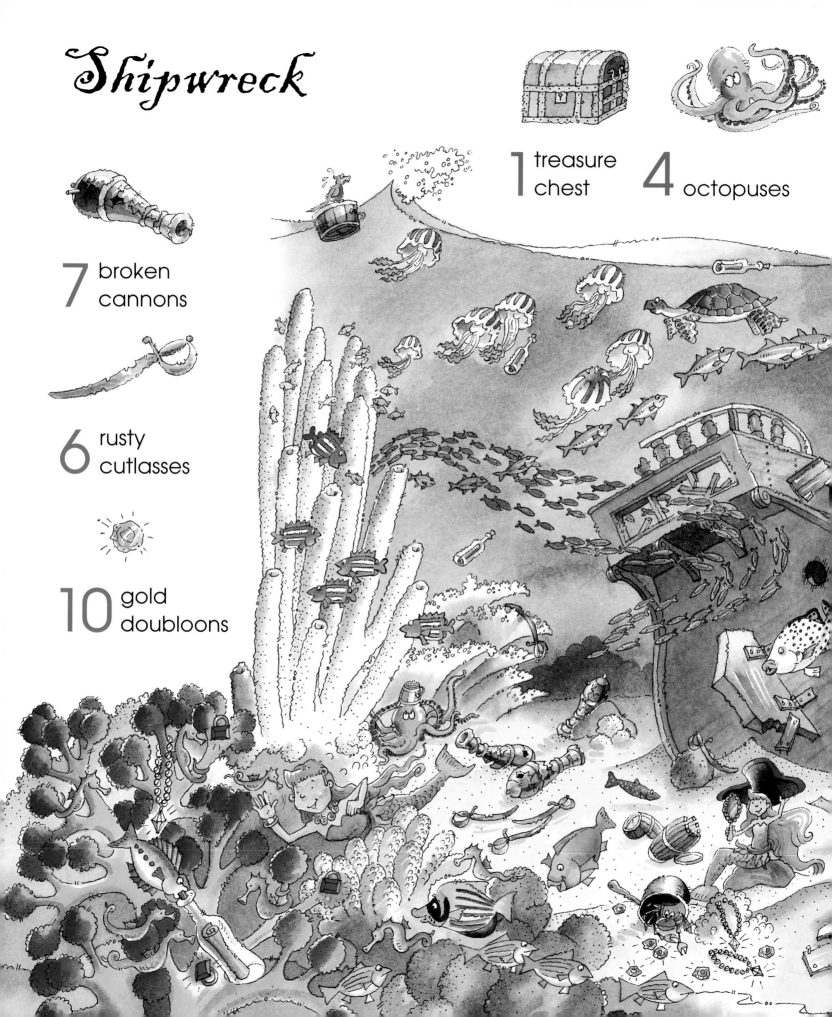

1 treasure chest

4 octopuses

7 broken cannons

6 rusty cutlasses

10 gold doubloons

9 mermaids 10 jellyfish 8 sea horses 5 messages in bottles 7 clownfish

Treasure hunt

Jack has found a wooden chest washed up on a beach. It's packed full of glittering treasure collected by the pirates on their adventures. Look back through the book and see if you can find and count it all.

7 silver tankards

10 gold bars

9 emeralds

5 golden compasses

6 pearls in shells

3 gold medals

9 silver spoons

7 conch shells

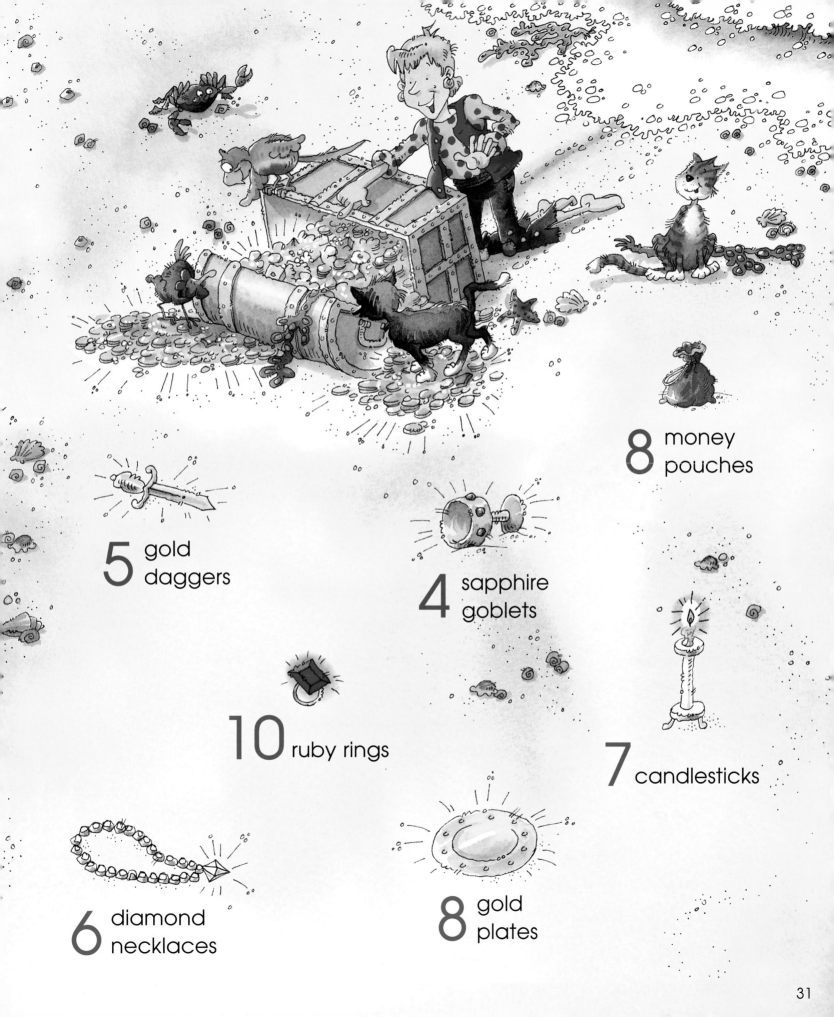

5 gold daggers

4 sapphire goblets

8 money pouches

10 ruby rings

7 candlesticks

6 diamond necklaces

8 gold plates

Answers

Did you spot all the treasure?
Here's where you can find it:

7 silver tankards:
The captain's feast
(pages 6-7)

9 silver spoons:
Pirate party
(pages 20-21)

10 ruby rings:
Shipwreck
(pages 28-29)

10 gold bars:
Keeping shipshape
(pages 10-11)

7 conch shells:
Treasure island
(pages 18-19)

7 candlesticks:
Ghost ship
(pages 24-25)

9 emeralds:
Stormy sea
(pages 26-27)

5 gold daggers:
Attack!
(pages 8-9)

6 diamond necklaces:
Shipwreck
(pages 28-29)

5 golden compasses:
Pirate school
(pages 14-15)

4 sapphire goblets:
Life at sea
(pages 4-5)

8 gold plates:
The captain's feast
(pages 6-7)

3 gold medals:
Pirate races
(pages 16-17)

8 money pouches:
Pirate port
(pages 12-13)

6 pearls in shells:
Monsters of the deep
(pages 22-23)

First published in 2007 by Usborne Publishing Ltd.,
Usborne House, 83-85 Saffron Hill, London EC1N 8RT, England. www.usborne.co.uk